The
Bar/Bat Mitzvah
Autograph
Book

Dearest Julie,
May this special
book capture your fondest
and most meaningful moments
of this cherished and
memorable occasion. We
love you! Congratulations!

Linda and Warren
Tyler & family

(March 1999)

The Bar/Bat Mitzvah Autograph Book

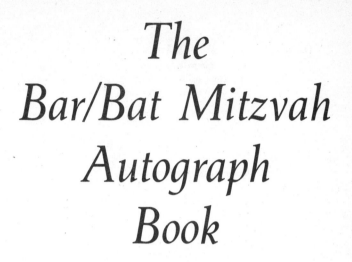

conceived and illustrated by

Miriam Seiden Novack

JASON ARONSON INC.
Northvale, New Jersey
London

For my husband, Harv,
who helps me believe in my dreams,
and for my parents,
Hugo and Natalie Seiden,
who awakened them in me

Interior design by Diane Berman

This book was set in 12-point Holland by Lind Graphics of Upper Saddle River, New Jersey, and printed by Haddon Craftsmen in Scranton, Pennsylvania.

10 9 8 7 6 5 4 3 2 1

Library of Congress Cataloging-in-Publication Data

Novack, Miriam.
    The bar/bat mitzvah autograph book / conceived and illustrated
by Miriam Novack.
    p.   cm.
ISBN 1-56821-069-8
    1. Bar mitzvah. 2. Bat mitzvah. 3. Autograph albums. I. Title.
BM707.N6 1993
296.4'424—dc20   93-13991

Manufactured in the United States of America. Jason Aronson Inc. offers books and cassettes. For information and catalog write to Jason Aronson Inc., 230 Livingston Street, Northvale, New Jersey 07647.

Dear Bar/Bat Mitzvah,

I originally designed this book for my own son, David, on the occasion of his Bar Mitzvah. I wanted to create a book that would give each of our friends and relatives the opportunity to share their thoughts and best wishes with him. Hoping to design a book that was both practical and creative, I illustrated some of David's and my daughter Michelle's favorite Bible stories and Judaic images. I then alternated these with pages for autographs. Also included were pages for the Bar/Bat Mitzvah's name, photo, and details from the special day.

This book was a gift of love that I shared with my son. Now I am happy to make it available to you, so that you too may have a memento of your very own day to share with your loved ones.

Mazel Tov,

Miriam Novack

(Place photo here)

Name __Julie Anne Dunitz__

Hebrew name __Devorah Miriam__

Named after __Dorthy Whitebook__

Birthday __3/26/86__
         (English date)   *(Hebrew date)*

Born in __Rochester, Minn.__
              (place)

Live in __Tulsa, OK__
           (place)

Attend __Temple Israel__ Religious School

My religious school teacher is __Cantor Levson__
                                (name)

My Own Thoughts on
Being a Bar/Bat Mitzvah

My Bar/Bat Mitzvah took place on __3/27/99__
(date)

at ___Temple Israel___
(name of synagogue)

My Torah portion was __Izav Levitucas ch 6 vs. 1-11__
(name of Torah portion)

My Haftarah portion was _____
(name of Haftarah portion)

My rabbi was ___Sherman___
(name)

My cantor was ___Lenson___
(name)

My reception took place at __Temple Israel__
(location)

on __3/27/99__
(date)

I had __275__ people help share my joy.

My Speech

This is a summary of my speech.

_____

_____

_____

_____

_____

_____

_____

_____

_____

_____

_____

_____

_____

_____

_____

_____

_____

_____

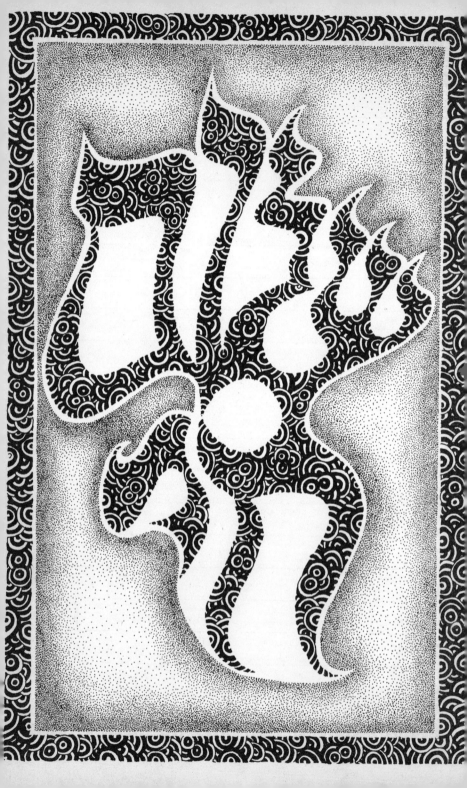

Dear Julie,

I can't tell you how proud Gramma and I are of you and of the beautiful performance you did today.

We love you!

Grandpa Moskowitz

Grandma M.

"If there is no justice, there is no peace."
Rabbi Bahya b. Asher

3/27/99

Dear Julie — this was a wonderful week-end. You were superb! Natalee Benstat

Julie —
Thank you so much for including me in your Bat Mitzvah celebration. This family gets better with each generation!
Mazel Tov — you were terrific!
Judy Tobk

Julie,
We loved sharing this beautiful moment of your life. Thank you for a lovely week-end —
Shirley & Howard Hochman

"And when the woman saw that the tree was good for food, and that it was a delight to the eyes, and that the tree was to be desired to make one wise, she took of the fruit thereof, and did eat, and she gave also unto her husband with her, and he did eat."

Genesis 3:6

Dear Julie,
    We're so proud
of you. You did
a fabulous job.
We're so happy
to be here in
Tulsa.
    We will look
forward to you
coming too Newton
to visit.
    Much good
health & happiness

        Love, Sid.
    Uncle Jerr
    aunt Jerr
    & Cousin Jeffrey

"In Thy light do we see light."
Psalm 36:10

Mazel Tov Julie,
You did a great job!

Shira M.

Great job
Julie! You should
be proud.
Stacy H

Julie!
You did such
a wonderful job!
We're so happy we
were able to help you
celebrate
your cousin,
Debbie Marks

"The Lord spoke unto Moses face to face."
Exodus 33:11

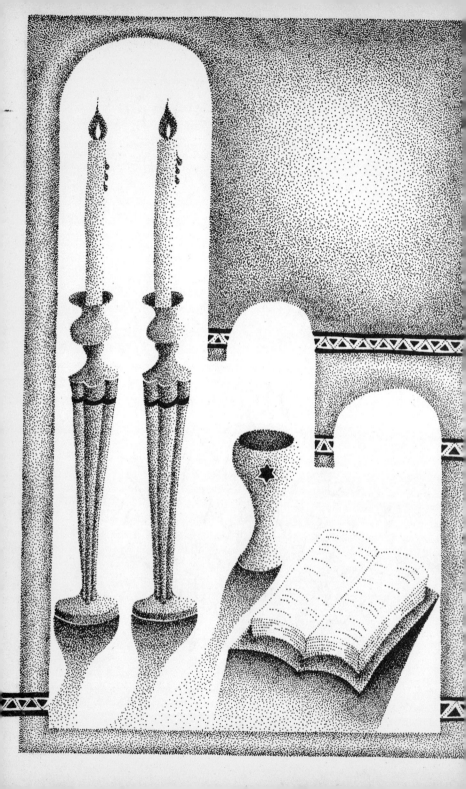

Julie;
Juice;
MAZel TOU
You did A greAt
Job This morning; I
know you would; I Also
Think iT was cool what you
said about All your grandparents
in your speech I AM very proud
To be your uncle I look forward
To seeing what you will Accomplish

Love Jimmy

"The Sabbath is the choicest fruit and flower of the week, the Queen whose coming changes the humblest home into a palace."

Rabbi Judah Halevi

Our dear ~~Julie~~! ✶ I tried to make your name artsy and think I overdid it.

Wow! What an incredible job you did today during your Bat Mitzvah! And what an incredible person you are — so self assured, so beautiful, so COOL! I totally love being your cousin and wish we could see each other more. But it's times like this one — mitzvahs when we can all be together — that are more than a Bat Mitzvah — ~~they is~~ it is a happening, a reunion of family & friends. We look forward to more mitzvahs with you & your family. Mazel Tov!

With love,
Linda, Warren & Melissa

"Who sets his eyes on what is not his, loses also what is his."

Sotah 9a

To our special Jalee

You were (and are)
so terrific —
Great Job!

Love - Aunt Kay

"Who prays without knowing what he prays, does not pray."
Rabbi Maimon b. Joseph

To my dear namesake Julie Ann

Way to go kiddo! You did a fabulous job on your Bat Mitzvah—

So glad I could be a part of it—

Julie A—

"We must not kill in vain even a snake or a spider."
Rabbi Zvi Hirsch Koidonover

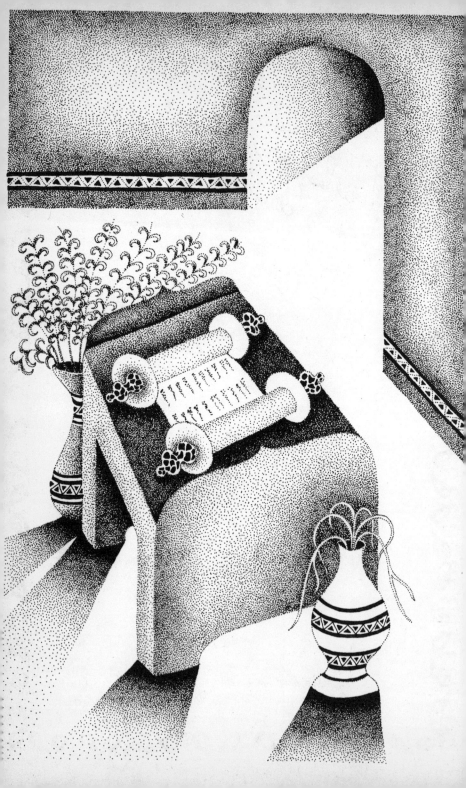

Julie —
Thank you for including us on your special day! You did a wonderful job. I'm sure you'll have many wonderful memories of your Bat Mitzvah weekend!
Rob Robert

Julie —
It's been a great weekend + a lot of fun! You will look back years from and treasure this weekend!
All the best
Cousin Mitchell

"When a man departs this life, neither silver nor gold nor jewels accompany him, only Torah and good deeds."

Rabbi Jose b. Kisma, the Mishnah

Julie,
You were ~~●~~ truly a great rally point for the entire family. Good Luck, and, Don't give up the piano!

      Leslie (who belongs to Stacy, who belongs to Toby & Gordon)

Julie,
    We had a great time! Thanks for bringing the family together once again. Good job at the service!!!

      Love,
      Joe, Debbie, Amy & Jon
      MARKS

"The Lord preserveth the faithful."
Psalm 31:24

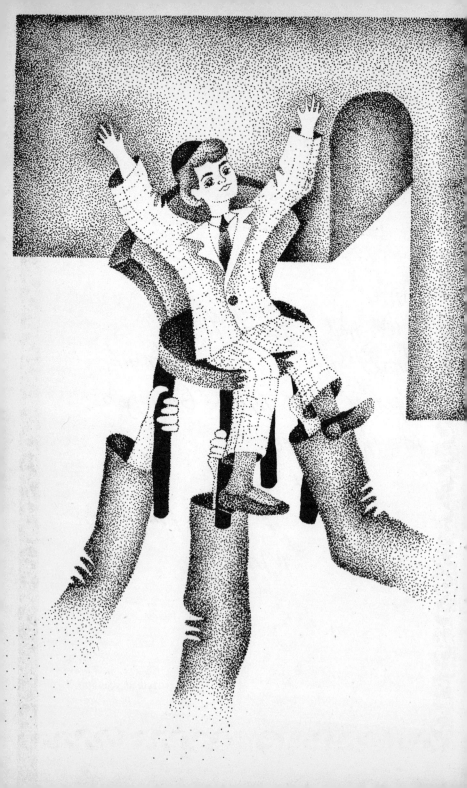

Julie,

Normally, I'd write long, flowing, poetic verses in which I'd sing your praises across many pages. Unfortunately, however, I've eaten too many of those wonderful sunday morning breakfast burritos, and as a result, lost my ability to write such an epic. So how 'bout I just say that you did a great job, and it was nice to see you again... and I'll probably see you soon again. I hope this bit of silliness gave you a good laugh.

Jeffrey

Julie!

You were great. We haven't heard a better performance for a bat mitzvah. We hope to see you at Jon Marle's bar mitzvah in April 2000.

Love,

Aunt Toby and Uncle Gordon
(Newman)

"And Jacob loved Rachel; and he said: 'I will serve thee seven years for Rachel thy younger daughter.'"

Genesis 29:18

"I will make of you a great nation."
Genesis 12:2

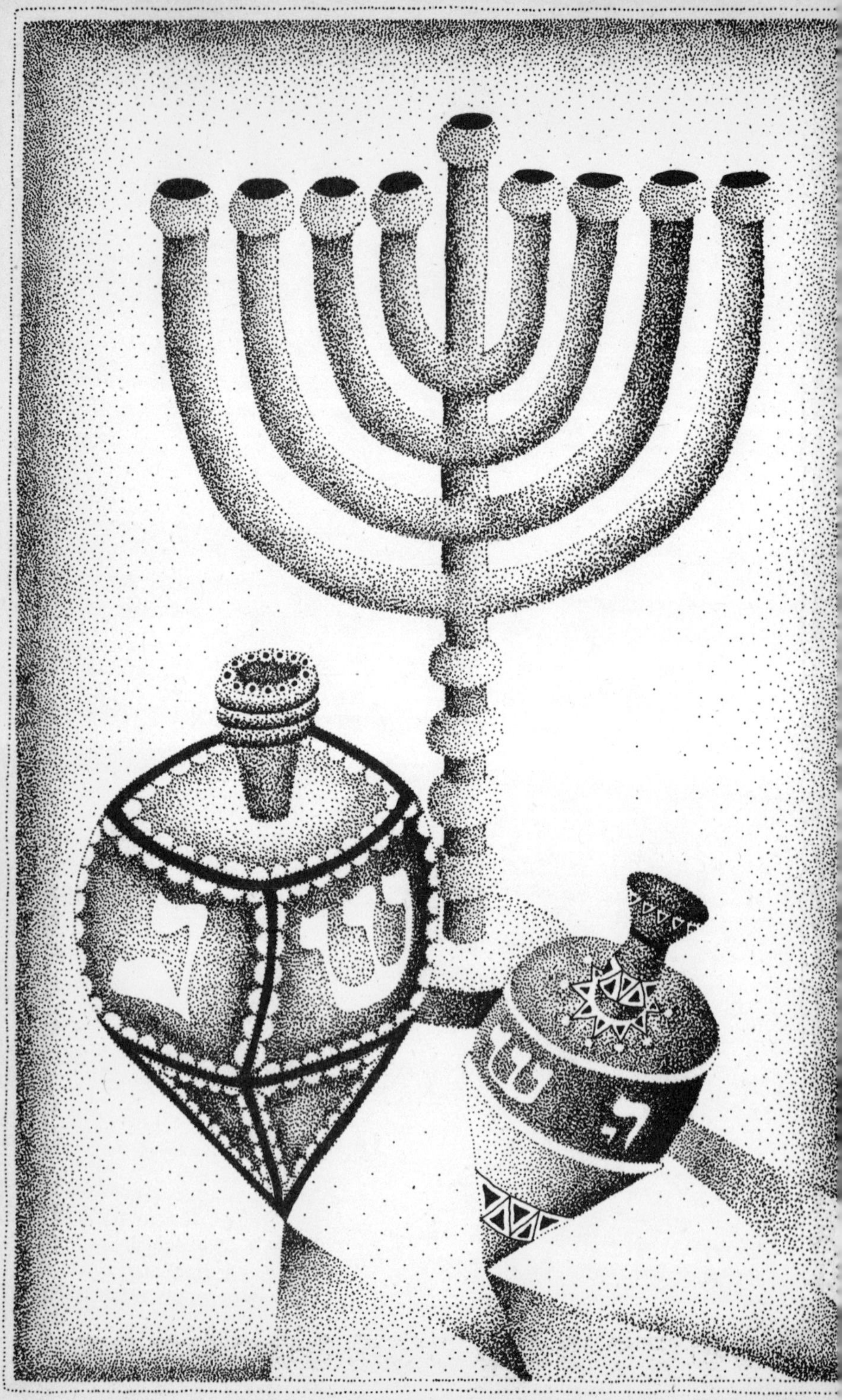
ש ג
ש ג

Dear Sweet Julie

You are so wonderful.
I feel very honored to
be your Aunt. Your fun
and you funny. It's a
great combination. Watching
you grow up is a real
treat. I also love the
fact that you and Daniel
are so close. Remember,
you always have your
Aunt Deanna. When you
need good advise (or Bad)
You can come to me.
I Love You

"Rejoicing on a festival is a religious duty."
Rabbi Joshua b. Hanania, the Talmud

Deanna

Hey Jules,

We were so proud of you all weekend! You may be in the middle, but there was nothing middling about your performance and poise and alacrity. Wow! Now that you're a full grown woman, you should be able to make your mom and dad bring you all to Southern California for vacation. Hope to see you there real soon.

Love, Bob and Laurie / Claire and Abby

"If I forget thee, O Jerusalem, let my right hand forget her cunning. Let my tongue cleave to the roof of my mouth, if I remember thee not, if I set not Jerusalem above my chiefest joy."

Psalm 137:5

Julie, dear,
You have
reached a real milestone!
Your family is so proud of
you for choosing to become a
Bat Mitzvah.
We have really enjoyed
spending time with you ~ first at
Brian's Bar Mitzvah, & now at
your own. We look forward
to other future happy occasions
that we can spend with you.

May you be blessed
with happiness always & may
you be surrounded by the love
of family & friends throughout
your life as you were this
week-end.   Love,
                 Cousins Elaine,
                 Michael, Brian,
                 Ruthanne, &
                 Jesse

"In each generation every man must regard himself as though he
personally had gone forth from Egypt."

The Mishnah

Dearest granddaughter Julie,

It was such a pleasure to be with my wonderful granddaughter.. You beautified this weekend for me and everyone by performing so eloquently and lovely.

I was so privileged to be in the ceremony and participate in everything.

Everyone raved what a wonderful time they had and also how good it was to see all the family and friends together.

Thank you for being so sweet and kind to me. I love you. Your parents, brother and sister very much.

You made me very happy

Love Grandma Em

Dear Julie,
I did not get to talk to you as much as I would have liked to. Hope at another time this will be possible.

My wish for you is to have much happiness and everlasting love and whatever your heart desires... Have a good life and best of everything.

Love —
Aunt Lil.

"We are not defenders of the wall, but the wall itself, and each and every one of us is a living brick of this wall."

Chaim Arlosoroff

Dearest Julie,

Nana & I are so proud of you — and we love you so very much!

You handled your Bat Mitzvah with so much charm and warmth, and with outstanding ability. Everyone loved the weekend and were impressed with you.

Love always,
Papa Unnie

"I have set before you life and death, the blessing and the curse; therefore choose life."

Deuteronomy 30:19

Dear Julie Anne,

Papa Normie and I are "bursting our buttons" over your performance.

You not only delivered with exceptional articulation and aplomb but a beautiful voice and incredible sweetness. And you looked so beautiful doing it.

We love you, darling, and wish only the best for you your whole life. May all your years be as sweet as this week-end.

Nana

"Then Moses said to the people, 'Commemorate this day, the day you came out of Egypt, out of the land of slavery, because the Lord brought you out of it with a mighty hand.'"

Exodus 13:3

"And David reigned over all Israel; and David executed justice and righteousness unto all his people."

2 Samuel 8:15

"Honor thy father and thy mother."
Exodus 20:12 and Deuteronomy 5:16

"Samson said, 'Let me die with the Philistines!' Then he pushed with all his might, and down came the temple on the rulers and all the people in it."

Judges 16:30

"The whole world is nothing more than a singing and a dancing before the Holy One, blessed be He. Every Jew is a singer before Him, and every letter in the Torah is a musical note."

Rabbi Nathan b. Naphtali Herz

"Who train themselves in wisdom cultivate true courage."
Philo

"Blessed is he who keeps the foundations of his fathers."
2 Enoch 52:9

"Come, let us build . . . a tower, with its top in heaven, and let us make us a name."

Genesis 11:4

"We blow a ram's horn to recall the Binding of Isaac."
Rabbi Abbahu, the Talmud

"A land flowing with milk and honey."
Exodus 3:8

"Friendship—one heart in two bodies."
Joseph Zabara

"Then Pharaoh's daughter went down to the Nile to bathe, and her attendants were walking along the river bank. She saw the basket among the reeds and sent her slave girl to get it."

Exodus 2:5

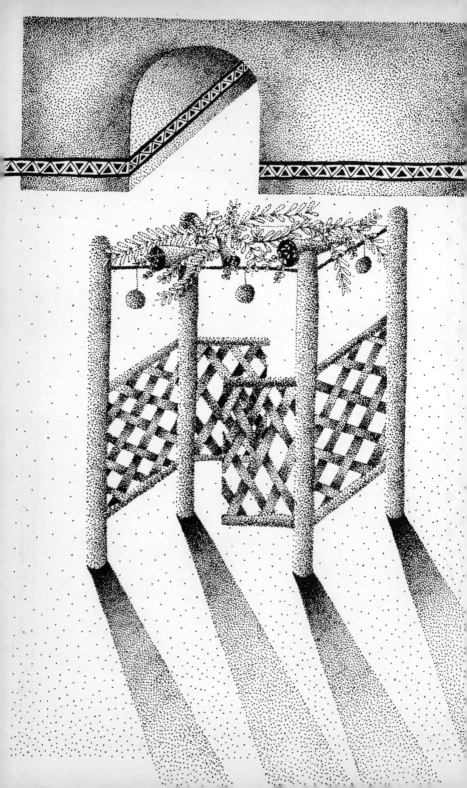

"*Joyfulness is the outcome of holiness. Therefore Sukkot, coming after Yom Kippur when we become holy and sinless, is called 'the season of our joy.'*"

The Kotzker Rebbe

"O bush, O bush! Precisely because you are the lowest of trees did the Holy One reveal Himself in you."

Rabbi Aha b. Raba, the Talmud

"When Haman saw that Mordecai bowed not down . . . he sought to destroy all the Jews."

Esther 3:5f

"Let them make Me a sanctuary that I may dwell among them."
Exodus 25:8

"The Jewish heroes were not men of battle, but men of faith."
Rabbi Moses Gaster

"Only he whose thoughts are pure, who shuns sin and is modest in his manners deserves to be king."

Isaac Abravanel

"Like the ants, the Jews never lose faith in life. . . . Hamans and Hitlers everywhere; yet they live on, and enjoy life."

Leon Berenson

"The voice is the voice of Jacob. The hands are the hands of Esau."
Genesis 27:22

"*Your name shall be called . . . Israel, for you have striven with God and with men, and have prevailed.*"

Genesis 32:29

"Thou shalt have no other gods before Me."
Exodus 20:3 and Deuteronomy 5:7

"So the people shouted, and the priests blew with horns. And it came to pass, when the people heard the sound of the horn, that the people shouted with a great shout, and the wall fell down flat, so that the people went up into the city, every man straight before him, and they took the city."

Joshua 6:20

"Thou, O Lord, art a shield about me."
Psalm 3:4

"We thank Thee for the miracles which You performed for our ancestors in those days."

Adapted from the Hanukkah Shemoneh Esrei

"When Israel crossed the Red Sea, the angels were about to break forth in song, but the Holy One rebuked them: My children [Egyptians] are drowning, and ye would sing?!"

Rabbi Johanan b. Nappaha, the Talmud

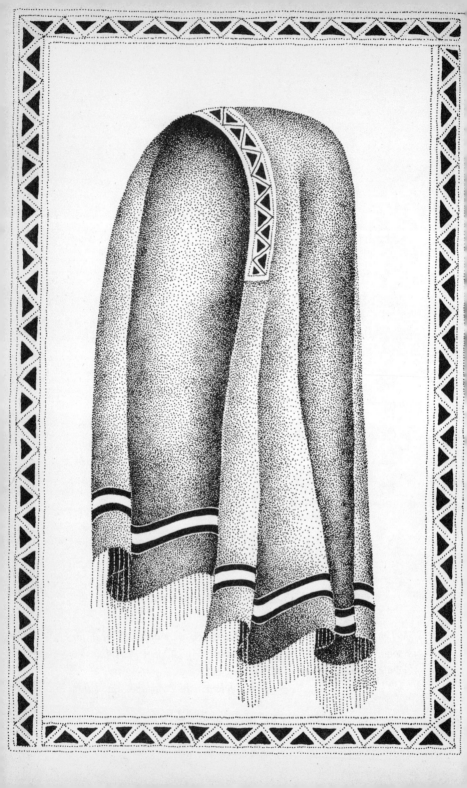

*"Let them make . . . fringes in the corners of their garments, and put
with the fringe . . . a thread of blue . . . that ye may look upon it and
remember the commandments of the Lord."*

Numbers 15:38f

"When morning came, there was Leah! So Jacob said to Laban, 'What is this you have done to me? I served you for Rachel, didn't I? Why have you deceived me?'"

Genesis 29:25

"Desire fulfilled is a tree of life."
Proverbs 13:12

Guests